Prime Time Plays

FOOTBALL'S SICKEST SACKS!

by Shawn Pryor

CAPSTONE PRESS
a capstone imprint

Capstone Captivate is published by Capstone Press, an imprint of Capstone.
1710 Roe Crest Drive, North Mankato, Minnesota 56003
www.capstonepub.com

SPORTS ILLUSTRATED KIDS is a trademark of ABG-SI LLC. Used with permission.

Library of Congress Cataloging-in-Publication Data
Names: Pryor, Shawn, author.
Title: Football's sickest sacks! / by Shawn Pryor.
Description: North Mankato, Minnesota : Capstone Press, 2021. | Series: Sports illustrated kids prime time plays | Includes index. | Audience: Ages 8-11 | Audience: Grades 4-6 | Summary: "Hike! When the center snaps the ball, the defensive line pounces, and it's prime time on the gridiron. From bone-rattling hits to game-changing take-downs, experience the sickest sacks from football's biggest superstars. These tremendous quarterback-crunching plays will leave you stunned!"—Provided by publisher.
Identifiers: LCCN 2020025086 (print) | LCCN 2020025087 (ebook) | ISBN 9781496695321 (library binding) | ISBN 9781496696892 (paperback) | ISBN 9781977154248 (pdf)
Subjects: LCSH: Football—History—Juvenile literature. | Tackling (Football)—Juvenile literature.
Classification: LCC GV950.7 .P79 2021 (print) | LCC GV950.7 (ebook) | DDC 796.332—dc23
LC record available at https://lccn.loc.gov/2020025086
LC ebook record available at https://lccn.loc.gov/2020025087

Image Credits
AP Images: ASSOCIATED PRESS, 25, Julio Cortez, 8, Nick Wass, 11, Ryan Kang, 7; Dreamstime: Jerry Coli, 14; Getty Images: Adam Bettcher, 28, 29, Focus On Sport, bottom 13, 19, bottom 21; Newscom: Arnie Sachs - CNP, top 21, David Maialetti, 10, Ray Stubblebine, 26, Rob Tringali SportsChrome, 23; Shutterstock: Alex Kravtsov, Cover, BK_graphic, design element; Sports Illustrated: Andy Hayt, 22, Chuck Solomon, 4, Heinz Kluetmeier, 16, John Biever, 5, Neil Leifer, top 13, Walter Iooss Jr, 15, 17

Editorial Credits
Editor: Christopher Harbo; Designer: Sarah Bennett; Media Researcher: Eric Gohl; Production Specialist: Katy LaVigne

All internet sites appearing in back matter were available and accurate when this book was sent to press.

TABLE OF CONTENTS

Words in **bold** are in the glossary.

SACK ATTACK!

It's fourth and six. Ten seconds remain on the game clock. The quarterback knows he must get the ball into the end zone for a win. He takes the snap and drops back. With time running out, he looks right and then left. He spots an open receiver. As he cocks back to throw—WHAM! A **defensive end** slams him to the ground from behind! Just like that, a shot at victory turns to defeat!

New York Giants defensive end Michael Strahan forces a fumble with a crushing sack of Washington quarterback Tony Banks during a 2007 matchup.

Minnesota Vikings defensive end Jared Allen (69) takes down Arizona Cardinals quarterback Kurt Warner in 2009.

Few plays in sports are quite like sacks. They keep quarterbacks on their toes and can change a game in an instant. They are also some of the most exciting plays in the National Football **League** (NFL). From sack **pioneers** to modern-day sack masters, get ready for the hits that shook quarterbacks to their souls. These are football's sickest sacks!

CHAPTER 1

CRUNCH-TIME SACKS

Crunch-time plays can change the direction of a game. Check out how these big-time sacks made a difference when it mattered most!

Electric Watt

Houston Texans defensive end J.J. Watt spent most of 2019–20 hurt on the sidelines. But he made a big-time return in a 2020 playoff game against the Buffalo Bills. The Texans were down 13–0 in the third quarter. At the same time, Bills quarterback Josh Allen had marched his team down to the 12-yard line. If the Bills scored a touchdown, the Texans' season could be over.

But Watt wasn't about to give up. On third and eight, Allen took the snap. As he dropped back, Watt rounded the edge of the offensive line. Before Allen could throw the ball, Watt slammed him to the ground! The sack forced the Bills to settle for a field goal. With the shift in **momentum**, the Texans went on a 22–3 scoring run to win in overtime.

J.J. Watt topples Buffalo Bills quarterback Josh Allen to turn the tide of a 2020 Wild Card game in the Texans' favor.

Clowney Crunch

When it comes to crunch-time sacks, Seattle Seahawks defensive end Jadeveon Clowney knows when to make them. In a 2020 Wild Card game, the Philadelphia Eagles needed a touchdown and a two-point conversion to tie the game. With the fourth-quarter clock running down, Eagles quarterback Josh McCown pushed his offense downfield. Only Clowney and the other Seahawks defenders stood in their way.

On the 10-yard line, McCown took the snap on fourth down. As McCown stepped up in the pocket, Clowney powered past an Eagles lineman. Just as McCown was about to make a play, Clowney landed a crushing sack. The crunch-time play gave the Seahawks the ball and the win!

Jadeveon Clowney wraps up Eagles quarterback Josh McCown to help give the Seahawks a 2020 Wild Card win.

Super Bowl Slam

In 2018, Eagles defensive end Brandon Graham made the biggest play of his **career**. With just 2:16 left on the clock in Super Bowl LII, the Eagles led the New England Patriots 38–33. Even though things looked good for the Eagles, New England's quarterback, Tom Brady, was leading a drive up the field.

Brandon Graham collides with Patriots quarterback Tom Brady, forcing a game-changing fourth-quarter fumble in Super Bowl LII.

On second and two from the New England 33-yard line, Brady took the snap. As he dropped back to pass, Graham fought through the Patriots' linemen. Just as Brady cocked his arm, Graham slapped the ball away and sacked him! The Eagles pounced on the **fumble** and took advantage of the turnover. With a game-clinching field goal, the Eagles won their first Super Bowl!

Helmet Popper

In a 2019 preseason game, Kenny Young of the Baltimore Ravens sacked Jacksonville Jaguars quarterback Gardner Minshew. The clean hit was so hard, Minshew's helmet popped off. Now that's sick!

CHAPTER 2

SACK PIONEERS

Before 1982, the NFL didn't keep official sack **statistics**. But that doesn't mean sacks didn't happen. Just ask any quarterback who faced these sack masters!

The Original Sack Master

Deacon Jones was a **legendary** defensive end. Not only did he help invent the pass rush, but he also coined the phrase "sacking the quarterback."

Early in his career, Jones joined forces with Los Angeles Rams teammates Lamar Lundy, Merlin Olsen, and Rosey Grier. The four were known as the Fearsome Foursome for good reason. They wreaked **havoc** on quarterbacks and offenses. By 1967, Jones was mowing down quarterbacks left and right. In his seventh NFL season, he was a sack-making machine. In just a 14-game season, he unofficially racked up 26 sacks!

Deacon Jones (75) pounces on running back Tucker Frederickson in a 1968 game between the Los Angeles Rams and the New York Giants.

FACT

During a 14-year career, Jones was a
league Defensive Player of the Year twice.
He was a first-team All-Pro defensive
end five times. He also entered the Pro
Football Hall of Fame in 1980.

Marvelous Martin

Harvey Martin once said his style of pass rushing was to "combine speed with 250 pounds and squeeze." This tough-as-nails Dallas Cowboys defensive end was a superstar during the 1970s and 1980s. Years before the NFL kept sack stats, Martin's numbers would have made most of today's defensive players jealous.

Harvey Martin sacks Tampa Bay Buccaneers quarterback Doug Williams during a 1982 NFC Divisional Playoff game.

FACT

In 1977–78, Martin was NFL and National Football Conference (NFC) Defensive Player of the Year. He also shared the Super Bowl Most Valuable Player (MVP) award with teammate Randy White.

During the 1977–78 regular season, Martin unofficially recorded 23 sacks and helped lead his team to the Super Bowl. In that big game, Martin sacked Denver's quarterback, Craig Morton, twice! He also deflected a pass and put pressure on Morton to throw four **interceptions**. The end result was a 27–10 Cowboys victory.

Staubach Stuffer

L.C. Greenwood was a key part of the Pittsburgh Steelers' famed "Steel Curtain" defense. The six-time Pro-Bowler played defensive end for 13 seasons. In 170 games, Greenwood unofficially recorded 73.5 sacks. On top of that, he forced 14 fumbles.

L.C. Greenwood

The biggest game of Greenwood's career took place in Super Bowl X on January 18, 1976. The Steelers squared off against future Hall of Famer Roger Staubach and the Dallas Cowboys. Greenwood was determined to help his team win. During the battle, he unofficially set a Super Bowl sack record. He took down Staubach four times on the way to a 21–17 Steelers victory!

FACT

In the NFL, a player earns a half sack when multiple players help him take down the quarterback.

L.C. Greenwood slams into Dallas Cowboys quarterback Roger Staubach during Super Bowl X in 1976.

CHAPTER 3

SACK LEADERS

What does it take to be a sack leader in the NFL? Big numbers and even bigger hits! From a terrifying team to standout super-sackers, these are some of the NFL's best.

The 1985 Chicago Bears

During the 1985–86 season, the Chicago Bears' defense was unstoppable. Their defensive **formation**, known as the "46 Defense," was loaded with top-notch defenders. They included Mike Singletary, Richard Dent, Wilber Marshall, Dan Hampton, Otis Wilson, William "Refrigerator" Perry, and many others.

Top-Ten All-Time NFL Official Sack Leaders

1. Bruce Smith: 200
2. Reggie White: 198
3. Kevin Greene: 160
4. Julius Peppers: 159.5
5. Chris Doleman: 150.5
6. Michael Strahan: 141.5
7. Jason Taylor: 139.5
8. Terrell Suggs: 139
9. DeMarcus Ware: 138.5
10. Richard Dent: 137.5
10. John Randle: 137.5

During the regular season, this defensive group led the league with 64 sacks. The team sack leader was lineman Richard Dent, with 17 sacks. The Bears' defense was so powerful it took the team all the way to Super Bowl XX. During their 46–10 blowout, they never let the New England Patriots' offense settle in. The Bears sacked their quarterback seven times!

Chicago Bears Dan Hampton (99) and Otis Wilson (55) double-team New England Patriots quarterback Tony Eason in Super Bowl XX.

Terrifying Taylor

In 1986, Lawrence Taylor proved he was one of the best defensive players of all time. That year, the New York Giants **linebacker** set a team record with 20.5 sacks. Among Taylor's best games was the week-eight matchup against Washington. In this crucial contest, the winner would take control of first place in the NFC Eastern **Division**.

During the game, Taylor was on fire. He recorded three key sacks to help give the Giants a 27–20 win. But that's not all. The Giants soon raced to a 14–2 regular-season record and a spot in the Super Bowl. Against Taylor and the rest of the Giants' defense, Denver quarterback John Elway never had a chance. The Giants beat the Broncos 39–20 in Super Bowl XXI.

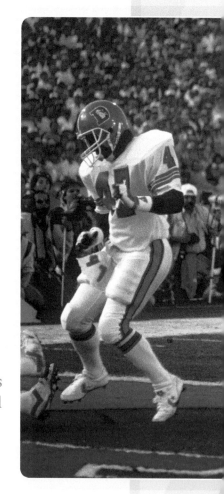

Lawrence Taylor cuts off Denver Broncos quarterback John Elway's path to the end zone during Super Bowl XXI.

Bone-Crunching Sack

Lawrence Taylor is also known for one of the most famous sacks of all time. On November 18, 1985, Taylor took down Washington quarterback Joe Theismann. It was a clean hit, but it snapped Theismann's leg and ended his NFL career.

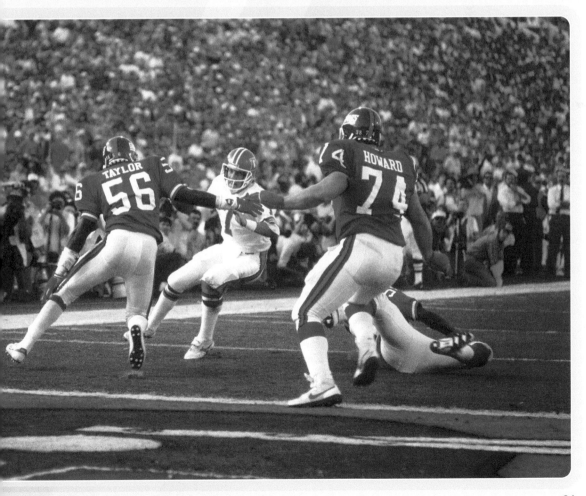

Wonderful White

Reggie White was a one-of-a-kind defensive wonder. The Hall of Famer led the league in sacks twice during his career. Nicknamed "The Minister of Defense," he racked up 198 sacks in 15 seasons. He was also a 13-time Pro-Bowler, two-time NFL Defensive Player of the Year, and eight-time All-Pro.

One of White's best seasons came in 1987. That year, a players' strike shortened the regular season, and White only played in 12 games. But that didn't stop him. In those 12 games, he sacked the quarterback 21 times! He even had multiple games with two or more sacks.

Reggie White
drives Indianapolis
Colts quarterback
Jack Trudeau into
the turf with a
bone-rattling sack.

FACT

During his career, Reggie White
recorded four sacks in a game
three times!

CHAPTER 4

RECORD-BREAKERS

Records are a badge of honor in the NFL. Here are just a few remarkable record-holders for taking quarterbacks to the turf!

Seven Sack Sensation

Known for his speed and strength, Derrick Thomas was a legendary linebacker. The Kansas City Chiefs star sacked the quarterback 126.5 times in his 11-year career. He was also a Pro Bowl player nine years in a row, from 1989 to 1997.

As a sack master, Thomas also had one of the greatest games of all time. On November 11, 1990, he sacked Seattle Seahawks quarterback Dave Krieg seven times in one game! One sack even knocked the ball out of Krieg's hands and led to an automatic touchdown in the end zone for the Chiefs. Although the Chiefs still lost the game, Thomas had a day for the ages.

Derrick Thomas stuffs Denver Broncos quarterback John Elway during a 1989 matchup.

Strahan's Record-Breaker

Michael Strahan was one of the best pass rushers in New York Giants history. He spent 15 seasons in the NFL, but the Hall of Famer's most memorable one came in 2001–02. As the regular season came to an end, he closed in on the single-season sack record. That record, set by Mark Gastineau in 1984, sat at 22.

When the Giants faced the Green Bay Packers on January 5, 2002, Strahan had racked up 21.5 sacks. He just needed one more to break the record. In the fourth quarter, Packers quarterback Brett Favre took the snap and dropped back. As he rolled to the right, Strahan pounced! To avoid a punishing hit, Favre began to slide as Strahan took him to the ground. With 22.5 sacks, Strahan had broken the record!

Michael Strahan flattens Green Bay Packers quarterback Brett Favre to capture a record-breaking 22.5 sacks in 2002.

FACT

Strahan's sack record is not without **controversy**. Some people think Favre gave up on the play on purpose and handed Strahan the record.

Two-Team Titan

Jared Allen excelled at finding the quarterback—a lot! During the 2011–12 season, he barreled full-tilt toward Michael Strahan's single-season record of 22.5 sacks. In the last regular-season game, he sacked Chicago Bears quarterback Josh McCown 3.5 times. His effort set the Minnesota Vikings' single-season franchise record. He wound up just a half sack shy of Strahan's record.

Jared Allen takes down Chicago Bears quarterback Josh McCown to set a Minnesota Vikings franchise record with 22 sacks in a single season.

Although Allen didn't overtake Strahan, he was a record-maker in a different way. He became the only other defensive player, besides Kevin Greene, to lead the league in sacks with two different teams. In addition to his league-leading 22 sacks with the Vikings, he had led the league with 15.5 sacks with the Kansas City Chiefs in 2007.

50 Fast!

During week 14 of the 2019–20 season, Minnesota Vikings defensive end Danielle Hunter made history. He sacked the Detroit Lions quarterback on the third play of the game. That sack was the 50th of his career. It made the 25-year-old the youngest player to ever reach 50 sacks.

GLOSSARY

career (kuh-REER)—the type of work a person does

controversy (KON-truh-vur-see)—a public disagreement or dispute between groups of people

defensive end (di-FEN-siv END)—one of two defensive football players positioned at the end of the linemen

division (duh-VI-zhuhn)—a group of people or teams in a certain category for a competition

formation (for-MAY-shuhn)—the way in which members of an offensive or defensive line are arranged

fumble (FUHM-buhl)—to drop the football while running with it

havoc (HAV-uhk)—great damage or chaos

interception (in-tur-SEP-shun)—a pass caught by a defensive player

league (LEEG)—a group of sports teams that play against each other

linebacker (LINE-bak-uhr)—a defensive football player who usually lines up behind the linemen but in front of the safeties

momentum (moh-MEN-tuhm)—a driving force gained by the development and unfolding of events

pioneer (PIE-uh-neer)—a person who goes before others, opening up the way for others

statistics (stuh-TISS-tiks)—the science of collecting numerical facts, such as a player's achievements on the field

READ MORE

Levit, Joseph. *G.O.A.T. Football Teams.* Minneapolis: Lerner Publications, 2021.

Lyon, Drew. *A Superfan's Guide to Pro Football Teams.* North Mankato, MN: Capstone Press, 2018.

Weakland, Mark. *Football Records.* Mankato, MN: Black Rabbit Books, 2021.

INTERNET SITES

The National Football League
www.nfl.com

Pro Football Hall of Fame
www.profootballhof.com

Sports Illustrated Kids
www.sikids.com

INDEX